I0798731

Students

LEVEL 7

/u/

DECODABLES

BY jump!

Teaching Tips

Turquoise Level 7

This book focuses on the grapheme **/u/**.

Before Reading

- Discuss the title. Ask readers what they think the book will be about. Have them support their answer.
- Ask readers to sort the words on page 3. Read the words together. Reinforce that /u/ can have a short /u/ sound or a long /u/ sound.

Read the Book

- Encourage readers to read independently, either aloud or silently to themselves.
- Prompt readers to break down unfamiliar words into units of sound and string the sounds together to form the words. Then, ask them to look for context clues to see if they can figure out what these words mean. Discuss new vocabulary to confirm meaning.
- Urge readers to point out when the focused phonics grapheme appears in the text. Does it have a short /u/ sound or a long /u/ sound?

After Reading

- Ask readers comprehension questions about the book. What were students in the book doing?
- Encourage readers to think of other words with the /u/ grapheme. On a separate sheet of paper, have them write the words into two columns: one under the short /u/ sound and the other under the long /u/ sound.

This edition is published by arrangement with Booklife Publishing.

North American adaptations © 2024 Jump!
5357 Penn Avenue South
Minneapolis, MN 55419
www.jumplibrary.com

Decodables by Jump! are published by Jump! Library.

Library of Congress Cataloging-in-Publication Data is available at www.loc.gov or upon request from the publisher.

ISBN: 979-8-88996-885-6 (hardcover)
ISBN: 979-8-88996-886-3 (paperback)
ISBN: 979-8-88996-887-0 (ebook)

Photo Credits

Images are courtesy of Shutterstock.com. With thanks to Getty Images, Thinkstock Photo and iStockphoto. Cover – PeopleImages.com - Yuri A. 4–5 – Ground Picture, Monkey Business Images. 6–7 – Studio Romantic, Drazen Zigic. 8–9 – wavebreakmedia, SeventyFour. 10–11 – Tom Merton, Monkey Business Images. 12–13 – fizkes, Monkey Business Images. 14–15 – Monkey Business Images, Gatot Adri. 16 – Shutterstock.

Can you sort these words into two groups? One group has **u** as in **unicorn**. One group has **u** as in **summer**.

bull

awful

human

tuba

pull

bush

super

Students are people who are educated on new things. If you have classes each week, whether with a teacher or on a computer, you are a student.

You do not have to stop being a student when you are an adult. You can keep being a student for as long as you want.

Some people think that being educated is so important that they spend several years getting a degree. A degree is proof that someone has been successful in a subject.

To help them get a degree, students may go to lectures. A lecture is a speech about a particular topic.

People who give lectures are experts in their subjects. Students often take notes so that they do not forget what the lecture is about. They will read their notes later to help them remember what was said in the lecture.

If students want to discuss a lecture, they might meet together on a campus. They can then compare their notes and go over points that people did not understand.

Campuses are shared spaces used by lots of students. Campuses are good places to find lots of people with shared interests.

Some campuses have places for students to relax when they are not at lectures. They may have student unions that run events or clubs for students to take part in.

To get a degree, students must first graduate. To do this, they need good grades on exams. Lots of students put their full focus into exams.

Exams may take place a few times a year or when new units of a curriculum are introduced. The curriculum is all the things that students will be instructed on. A unit is one part of the curriculum.

Exams come in different formats. Some students have to submit essays. Submit means to hand in. Some students have to demonstrate that they have picked up new skills in their subject, which they might do by playing a musical instrument.

If you are not sure what you will do in the future, that is OK. You have lots of time to think about it! Studying the right degree can be a good step in helping you do the things you want to do in the future.

Say the name of each object below. Is the "u" in each a long /u/ sound or a short /u/ sound?